Phallic Symbols

By Cletus Crow

C≡≡3

PIG ROAST PUBLISHING LLC.

Praise for Phallic Symbols

"Cletus Crow tackles the book-length-topic poetry collection with a deft voice and endless compassion. These poems are undeniably funny, but in no way is this debut work 60 Dick Jokes. Each page took my breath away."

– **Graham Irvin** author of Liver Mush and I Have A Gun

"In spite of its title, *Phallic Symbols* is more Jungian than Freudian: a journey into the collective unconscious that's as profound as it is scatological, full of powerful poems that are simultaneously mythic and modern, evoking universal spiritual desires even as they despairingly indulge in timeless obscenities. Call it *The Hero with a Thousand Dicks.*"

– **William Duryea** Editor in Chief of Misery Tourism

"*Phallic Symbols* is a harrowing, heartbreaking catalogue of erotic obsession, a howl of pain perched on the precipice of suicide. In surreal, pornographic poems that veer wildly between humor and agony, sacred and profane, [Cletus Crow] illuminates the dark, secret places where sex and madness converge. The Mona Lisa of dick poetry."

– **Miss Unity** Associate Editor of Hobart, author of Who Killed Mabel Frost?

Some of the poems have been featured in:
Hobart
HAD
Apocalypse Confidential
Forever Magazine
Funicular Magazine
Don't Submit
Back Patio Press
God's Cruel Joke Magazine
Misery Tourism
Spectra
Bizarre Publishing
ExPat Press
Rejection Letters
SCAB Magazine
SWAMP

Published by Pig Roast Publishing, LLC

www.pigroastpublishing.com

ISBN: 979-8-9891470-4-5

Hike with Erectile Dysfunction

Five flailing oak trees
stiffen toward the boy blue sky.
Their trunks lean like naked men
in gym locker rooms.
Each branch varies in length
shape and size.
Each leaf is an averted eye.

It's this spear I wield
as skin-thin divining rod
stumbling through forests soft
as flaccid flesh hangs low
like my head in frostbitten hands.

Dream

Our cat is flying
our dicks are huge
but the dream
is about the crucifixion.
We keep waiting
for Jesus to come back.
Jesus seldom comes back.
So we raise our kids
in dreamscape where
our cat is flying
our dicks are huge
but the dream
ends with gnashing teeth.
When I wake up
Jesus sleeps soundly
on the screened porch.
Our dicks are small

Seasonal Allergies

Asshole arborists
mostly plant male trees.
Population management:
because life can't happen
without paperwork.
The trees are horny.
They pollinate my eyes.
Yellow cum covers my car
and everything else.
Someone drew a smiley face
on the windshield.
Someone drew a penis.
Someone wrote "I love you"
on both headlights.

Mime

I can't break through imaginary glass.
Your voice is an outline
etched by my palms
when weeknights end in television.
Our Doberman barks at her reflection.
She's an animal
which means less than stupid.
I'm hairy like an animal.
You're a reflection
meaning kind of dead.
I trace the words ricocheted
like grenade shrapnel.
We'll never become our parents.
At Bonnaroo, you were proudly a girl
with photogenic penis,
waiting for another Bonnaroo.

Vacation

They should invent true happiness.
You feel nothing
perched on the Cliffs of Moher
beside the hung boyfriend.
They should make a way to jump
without dying
so you can feel air through your fur.
They should stuff that feeling
in a syringe,
but you feel like falling for real,
so they should invent God
or some massive net.
You feel yourself step forward.
They should let you do it,
but no one wants to ruin the moment.
There are kids here.
You're sorry for their open eyes.

Sunday

so good to just sit
in a hot car and sweat
after arguing
over who should empty the litter box

stepping out
july mimics autumn's auburn breeze
better than ecstasy

O cock O kitty pee
O malignant monogamous sex drive
pain pain pain
i'm immunized to our chaos

Soy Boy Snowflake Self-Hatred

Idk who to blame for all this caring.
You say you're scared of whales dying
and fundamentalist Christianity.
As a child, I was scared of cryptids,
quicksand and nuclear weapons.
Somehow, I'm more and less scared
of the dark lately.
I've always worried about getting raped,
which is weird because
I like being sexually dominated.
My relationship with fear is fuccboi-esque.
I was afraid of an X-girlfriend
until she blackmailed me with old dick picks,
threatening to post on Facebook
unless I bought her Louboutins.
We made up years ago.
Now, I'm scared of dying without enemies
because that's proof
of not really living your life.
I open my computer, the earth sobs
and it's impossible
to wash my eyes, say whatever.
As a weakling, I'm afraid of necessary pain.
I worry about disappointing my dad.
Idk who I need to kill to wake up.

Süchtig Werden

We haven't had sex in weeks,
but that's okay
since I don't feel anymore.

I'd rather jerk off,
alone,
to German torture porn.

Porn proves romance takes refuge:
violence as
intimacy's last resort.

Like maybe I'd burn myself
the fuck alive
just to kiss your spineless dick.

Ode to the Men's Room

To sharpie scrawl and piss-smeared stalls
To drawn dicks fucking assholes
And I know your girlfriend
For A+J 4ever and the alphabet in love
For sexual frustration
As shitty advice
And scribble scratched genitals
For boobs like circles
Bodies like sticks
Your smiling face of four lines
Privy to drunk encounters
To brave ten-digit sex workers
Rural gas stations and fast food thrones
To a good time one call away

Mosquito Penis

Nothing personal.
You taste as good as anyone,
and I want to live.
Palms crush our small skeletons.
The blood you see
is from whoever-previous-meal.
People forget
whose blood is on their hands.
Most of us live three weeks.
I want to be a concert pianist.
I fuck my wife.
She is a mosquito, too.

Vasectomy

you called me fickle
I was offended

arguments afterward
taste like dead kids

if someone snipped
my violin string

your ticket punched
shrugging silence

think how easy
the absence of poop

yet future selves
could see it as bone

we could need kids
to stay in love you say

haha funny joke
our black tea is cold

Bisexual Dystopia

Their guns shoot spermicide
every femboy contains the soul
of an aborted fetus
and my eyes were made in China.

In bedrooms across America
microscopic cameras ensure
no man has anal sex
with femboys or his iPhone.

We milk sacred femboys
to embolden hardiness and valor
as these balls are blue
symbolizing vigilance and justice.

Dressing colorfully will get you
exiled from paradise.
I mean it this time says Mrs. Officer.
Her breath smells like femboy.

BDSM

A whip hangs above
handcuffs on the doorknob.

You hate me correctly
at specified times.

Camping

Coyotes echo my inner dialogue.
Maybe one mauled a baby rabbit
and doesn't want to share.
No matter how much I love you
this tent is too small for two horndogs.
We smell like gasoline.
We got horny messed around
now there's no paper to wipe ourselves.
Your romantic misconception
of Tennessee wilderness
has fueled mosquito flight
my blood circulating through nature's
trickle-down economy.
Maybe I'd eat human feces
if it meant sucking your face hole
so I swallow itchiness
and pretend I'm the first-ever mammal
without hide fur or flesh.
I think about dad yelling "pussy!"

High on Life

I could walk down rusty train tracks
and never be seen again.

My tattoo of a centipede hurts
because it's new.

I'm thankful for all the pain
and all the flowers in this green world.

Fucking Walt Whitman:
I'd be one of those boys he loved.

You Grow to be Weightless

another wet dream
with Brad

the adolescent urge
to exist inside a dream

every adolescent-
what they cleave from guessing

i'm my mother my
father and innumerable
hot pockets

i'm time spent masturbating

as if time doesn't fly
it shoots

Health Freak

With a big, black
butt plug,
smoothie boy
mushes cucumbers
into whirring,
raising his hands
above where I wonder
about dipping
something flesh-soft,
seeing how quickly
it's destroyed
and if the boy's blender
loves like we do,
emulsification
until juice:
your favorite way
to consume me,
that nutrient
gifting you strength.

Uber Eats

How do we advertise
a dusty sepulcher?

You injecting innumerable lattes
with roses
as I deliver acai bowls
to quarantined psychiatrists.

It's when ramen slips
through the needle's eye.

Why our doppelgangers
have MFAs in necromancy
but can't afford shit.

Tonight, vegan parfaits
bulge out of my freezer bag
like big dicks in jeans.

Imagine we live where
I'm going: each moat filled
with crocodiles,
an unattainable mortgage.

Soft Boi

uummmm
we're sorta windshields

almost transparent

if i crash our bodies
they'll shatter most likely

our faces perhaps crack
in a kinda web

i've somewhat doomed
this churchy state

roaming for art baes
to ugh properly

myself a sentient dildo
uummmm yea

The Sons

My grandmother's firstborn
was a stillbirth.

I didn't know about it until yesterday.

She was massaging her upper thigh.

"Worse than after my stillbirth,"
she said to no one.

I think of tiny animals
squished by pickup trucks.

She was going to name him Cole.

It's my dad's name.

This Written on a Cave Wall

A ghost without a sheet is the breeze. Strong winds are a bunch of naked ghosts running a race. A tornado is when they get lost. Their tears are the rain, obviously. The sun is a big ghost on fire. The sky is the biggest ghost. His nail clippings are the moon most nights. The clouds are dandruff or cum.

Alternate Reality Where I Succumb to White Trash Instincts

It's like herding snakes
through a forest fire.

The homing pigeon
of misery
is my baby mama's
text message.

I make meth
with some man named Jesus
who is not God.

Life started
after dad shot our dog.

I have twelve dogs now.

Dream #2

They're filming my execution. You're about to cut my head off. The director yells cut. You're confused whether he means cut as in stop or cut as in cut. You hesitate. The studio shifts sideways. My head hinges from my neck. The director yells God fucking dammit. You peel off your hood, your rosy cheeks sweet with sweat. I don't need to bend to kiss you. I say suck my dick, cruel world, then walk through the wall.

Employed Again

Zero for it but to watch hentai and cum in a black sock.
The angel of death of American work ethic has abandoned
other twenty-something souls. Excess dopamine glows
molten plastic. Lethargic contentment kills chemical relief
hanging from my neuron cross with memory nails. "I had a
friend who lit his pants on fire because he didn't wanna go
to school or something. I don't know. He was basically
fine." I wish Waco had a happy ending. Heaven's Gate
better shoes. Ugh. Ah. Damn.

Transfiguration

i miss my
old fourteenth floor
apartment

no one could see
that high up

it was perfect
standing naked
in the window
on sunny days

this is how
vampires
kill themselves
i would think and
still be alive

Phallic Symbols

I wield my penis point up
so its cyclops eye
can imagine clouds as animals,
no thirst for blood,
only elephants and God.

My penis is innocent
and loves God,
the ultimate penis haver,
who has everything
so His penis is just what it is.

One day, I will gather
each shotgun,
guitar, lightsaber, limitation,
cucumber, balloon,
spear and shame.

I will push this sexy pile
down a volcano
so my penis can be just what it is:
just some troubled worm,
another brain
and a broken feeler
that reminds me of your teeth.

Dahmer Would Love Online Dating

i undress
boy zombies
in the mirror

black leather
part shadow
contorting like
a mime

it's time now
old twinks
were disposed of
but i'm tipsy

i can't eat
you and grandma
shivers
with her bag
of tradition

my bio reads
softness
makes me sick

you're sorry
we'll wake
without names

i pretend
our fathers
are dead
before kneeling

although shame
can be fun
in the right light

i scroll through
flesh searching
as if reborn

.

Museum Statue

no limbs

a small penis
represents wisdom
they claim

Catholic

you pray to Mary for misery
breaking bro code
we were spanked southern baptist
but admire the aesthetic
and history of medieval torture
young me hoped to be a youth pastor
just to be a long-haired youth pastor
just to be jesus hot
another unattainable otter
wearing birkenstocks
perusing megachurch sound systems
how we'd wave our arms
as shipwreck survivors
striving to catch the jumbotron's
invisible eye
or remember Grayson
tonguing my cheek
all that talk of how heaven
couldn't feel warmer/intimate
it's not fair
it's not fair
two days after beginning this poem
you met a wayward priest
he's obviously closeted
he has def done some shit too
and your art has gotten better

Dysmorphia

My penis
grows wings and flies into the sun
when I'm jealous of a beige mannequin's
crotch, its unfeeling smoothness.

I wish.

I wish it was as easy as words.

Sleepover

I propose a dick-measuring contest.

The loser must strip
completely naked
and run once around the block.

Mark grips his tighty-whitey waistband
like an elastic noose.

"What are you gay, Mark?" I ask.

Sam and Victor laugh. I'm an asshole.

Mark shuts eyes sheds shorts
and unleashes the biggest penis
I've ever seen
except for pornography.

"Your turn, asshole," Mark says seething.

The winter twilight
cools my erection like a snake
on some moss-slick boulder.

Final Boss

My sword is the size of a skyscraper.
My mouth is a dragon maw.
Your character dodges masterfully
before each strike.
This is the whole of existence
until you get good enough.
I will evaporate in a pearlescent cloud.
The cutscene showed
how we were lovers
but then came the warlock's curse.
I am the warlock and his curse.

The Masochistic Slug

If you need a shoulder to cry on. Oh baby. Yes. Just like that. It burns.

Near Future

The best part of having a cybernetic penis is it's also a gun.
The second is it can't malfunction. I cum inside, and the
bullet destroys his left lung. How could this happen? The
switch on my testicles is set to kill. The worst part of
having a cybernetic penis is it's easy to forget you have
one. The second is somehow, even without a cybernetic
penis, you would hurt the people you love.

Missiles Shaped like Eggplants

food penis water penis country penis guns penis fear penis
bombs penis us penis them penis hate penis propaganda
penis lies penis draft penis death penis the toes on my right
foot got crushed I don't know how I promise I'm not lying
penis it keeps me awake at night penis losing oneself to
history's recurring fuck you

Literary Society

There are too many words I don't know.

The poets are coming to kill me.

Spoiler for Boogie Nights

in the end
he hanged himself
with himself
but he was hung enough
already

Some Drunk Guy

wanna go in for beer so bad
nude afternoon with Nashville legs
red hair set pillowcase ablaze
couldn't get thang up pop Viagra
kinda blue stare through feet first
striding past oak thick roots
down sidewalk man huddled plastic
bags within are red blue cans
so know this too urban for happy
and wanna leave bad all them
farm East Tennessee masturbate
in peace for once live a lone
future corpse our arguments real
violent the thought don't sting
but feels good feel it cum enter
drink drown sorrow stagnated
my sweet and understanding bitch
even bought her best type cow
best type grapes now Jesus blood
ain't forgiven anal retentive ol
ass can't believe she wanted me
those innumerable months ago

Poem Written After Watching Tetsuo the Iron Man

I'm becoming a man
which is to say disfigured
beyond recognition.

My penis is a sewage pipe.

There are pieces of metal in my brain
called shame.
They attract pain like a magnet.

Silverware in the socket tickles.

Tenderness shocks me.
Roses burst from your chest
and I watch them die.

Let's make a dead new world.

"We'll rust this world into the dust
of the universe,"
you scream like a supervillain.

I can't get enough sex with hate.

I'm becoming a gun
which is to say an agent
of dramatic change.

The Night You Stormed Out

I had Smoky all to myself.
We watched Saw 2,
and she didn't budge during ultraviolence.
I drank four cans of PBR.
The ceiling was dingier than usual.
I'd never noticed its cracks,
how rain discolored waterlogged corners.
I tried to fuck the couch cushions.

Five-Minute Man

The cape got heavy
With constant cries for help
Flying is tiring
And smiling all the time
The tights seemed tight also
So he tossed them out
Tried a desk job
Worked Delivery Dudes
Unhappy Übermensch
Until he masturbated once
Without catching it
Sperm shot through the ceiling
Ceilings
Grazing a guy on floor ten
Piercing the sky
It burned up mid-atmosphere
Now Pornhub
Films cross-country facials
Where the woman's in Texas
And Five-Minute Man
Rubs one out in New York
People fucking love that shit
They bring their families on the lawn
Try spotting cum hurtling
Splat
He wears his cape
And nothing else
He is almost happy
After post-nut clarity
But can't turn off his ears

They Called Me a Pervert Monster

I die from tolling church bells.
I wear crop tops and red.
I only fuck sometimes
and am happy less than that.

I Love You

The ripped paper towel plastered with blue ink taped to the fridge reads: "I'm so tired of having sex with you! I wish you were more sadistic! I need someone to hurt me! We repeat the same three positions every night! I've told you I want BDSM stuff, but what do you ever do about it?" This after an unsuccessful blowjob. I read your text apology three hours later. "I love you so dearly, and I love having sex with you. There are times I wish it felt more sadistic or that we had sex in more positions (I know height plays into it). But that's it. With no anger in it, that's the only real issue. I don't think you're some limpdick hippie queer or ugly." I google "unique sex positions" and "how to be sadistic in the bedroom." I google "partner unhappy with vanilla sex" and "gay BDSM tips," which leads to Pornhub. Ads for sexual enhancement pills pop up at the top of the browser. I google "fish with the light bulb" because your anger reminds me of a deep-sea angular fish. You draw me in with insults, filling your belly when we're both crying. After days of googling, I learn enough to ask relevant questions. Do you want to be pissed on? Is knife play too edgy? Should I draw blood? Do you want to live alone in a cabin in a forest in Alaska? You'd become a memory. I could hurt you how you hope to be hurt, then. The sex dungeon in my head has many rooms. Weird that happiness can't exist without a bit of pain. I'm not talking about burning your thighs with candle wax.

Eternal Life

Methuselah died
at nine hundred
and sixty-nine, which
is enough if
only to get to know you.

The lack of longevity
available now
should be criminal.

I hold out hope
a fountain of youth
washes up
on Miami Beach,
seaweed cloaking
ornate gold.

We're young enough
for forever,
immortal like weather,
and hump softly
until this place becomes ash.

Performative Cannibalism

After apocalypse
you'll find me, a cannibal,
drooling down the roadside,
wearing intestines,
my face skin volcanic
from radiation.
A man and his son pass
like black cats across my path,
too far to skewer
but near enough to smell.
I haven't stopped writing about dicks.
My spear is a plastic
Christmas
tree.

Tokyo Burning

Godzilla does not have a penis.

Letter to OCD

Terrorists won't castrate you in a garage.

Flipping the light switch seven times will not dispel
demons
if there are demons.

And if there are demons, there are also angels.

You are not a serial murderer.

Testicular cancer isn't a case of blue balls
after watching someone hot walk down the street.

The consensual dick pics sent in college did not include
your face.

God is probably benevolent.

You do not transform into a wolf every full moon.

There are thousands of tomorrows most likely.

Morning rises like a god of pain.

Then comes a night with your penis in
the love of your life.

Still Alive

I'm dying of something inexorable.
The doctor says
death is a kind of fuccboi.
"And are you a stupid slut?" he asks.
Thankful for chastity lately.

Another Love Poem

I can't suck my own dick.
Remove a rib and maybe it's possible.
God stole Adam's rib and made Eve.
He ruined the world with someone to love.
You are more than one rib.
You are two hundred and six different bones.
Each day my life is ruined in new ways.
I love how your head smells addictive.
You suck my dick like hope.

Why I Hate Parties

shooting the breeze
with a gun

talking shit
and it's pouring out your mouth
in thick steaming clumps

please shut up man

let's drink beer silently
like you're my dad

Mercy

Jesus laughs at my gray pube,
but I can't see, hear or touch him.
I know Jesus exists.
Otherwise, I'd be pure like meth,
a purse filled with cyanide pills.
I know Jesus laughs.
He's drunk off his own blood,
and knows all pain.
I want to give birth before death.
I'll kill my children
if they know too much.
Every minute brings me closer,
near the annihilating answer.

God Also Made...

your squirrel nest wig
post drag show

purple silhouette
passing out poppers

that man skeleton

Slutty College Hunk with Huge Cock has Leg Shaking Orgasm

You started masturbating heavily
after all those people hated you.
It's not just frequency and amount
but your repeated
turning to porn for answers
it cannot provide.
The laptop screen is like amber
a mosquito got stuck in.
You bang against the glassy surface.
You want confrontation
with biblically accurate angels
but God is multiple friends
saying they love you
not quite using those words.
Your therapist claims admission
is the first and most important
most difficult step.
She suggests support groups.
The people pictured online
are photo-shopped
recently showered cardboard cutouts
with beautiful teeth.
Your teeth are yellow scum.
Still you'd like to smile
at least once during the day.
You raise the phone to your face
remember Dante walked through Hell
on his way to Heaven.
Lately Hell is lust without love.
Do you love yourself enough to change?

Moby Dick

After Graham Irvin

A whale's penis is eight to ten feet long. Whalers in the nineteenth century would skin it and make clothes. The fabric was said to be soft, stretchy and water resistant. "Hey, man, nice shirt." Thanks. It's penis. Anyway, my white whale is a shirt that cures depression.

Chiseled Jaw

wide eyes
the weight of blue
tearing up
to our white ankles

my mother sobs
because her wings are made
of pipe cleaners

when the jesus portrait
in the living room
grows legs
unnails itself
and watches me sleep
i realize silence
is how god speaks

he resembles an early 2000s
johnny depp

i try hiding my erection

please stop crying

Dildo

vibrating like
hate mail
from anonymous

kinda jealous
know i shouldn't be
but still

it's simply better
bigger
neon green silicon

the lightsaber
of old jedi masters
the sound too

as a big boy
i gorged star wars
with granddad

meek manhood
meat pizza
mom's not home

i wish my penis
could cut
through blast shields

recalling
oneself so innocent
bad headache

Outrageous Nowadays

Man offered to buy my old gym socks for $30.
Can you imagine?
$20 more and we can go see a movie.

Uncircumcised

My grandfather
in his cracked eighties
fallen in the shower
naked as a baby squirrel
because his skin's that pink.
The water had been scalding.

As a child,
he sprinted through my daydreams.
He coached high school football
for nineteen years and
could outrun the youngest stud,
flapping ears like wings
humongous like mine.

I shoot forearms under
his armpits, lace my fingers
and lift up trying not to gaze down:
origins no one should see.

After he's enveloped,
I carry him through the bedroom,
waiting for another vision
to change my life.

A ghost emerges glowing,
donning khaki shorts, a ruby jersey
and pearl tennis shoes,
and all of it beams silver.

"I want Elaine here
like a snake wants human legs,"
he says. Even the tenor
of his voice clatters like coins
dropped on the hardwood.

Washington Monument

skydiving
i'd land on it
ass first
and die
remembering you

Not Man Enough

Smokey died.
No taxidermist would stuff her.
I tried to do it myself
via YouTube tutorial
and failed.
Pink vase full of ashes.

Therapy

My therapist says
I should clone myself
so I can kill myself
without dying.

Only then, with my hands
around my neck, will I find
a reason to breathe.

My therapist says
whichever version of me
wins the fight
will be stronger for it.

Only then can I enjoy
sunsets, love my mom and
know I'm lucky I'm alive.

"You have the Ass of a Fully Grown Cherub"

When a cherub grows up,
he hates angels.
When a cherub grows up,
he loses wings,
swallows bright blue
antipsychotic medication,
and drives to PLAY Friday nights,
a gay club in Nashville, TN,
feeling invisible fingers of eyes
pinch his pert apple ass.
He was once a self-identified
sex and love addict
who couldn't stop smoking cigarettes.
Now, the cherub owns a cat.
He stays true to monogamous
romantic relationships.
He's been thinking about growing up
with a normal penis
and what that means for himself
and others born sinless yet into sin,
human humanity.
The cherub wants to know
if life gets easier,
whether any type of god loves
"like a hurricane."
He stares at his feet,
lights another menthol Marlboro.
When a cherub grows up,
he never does.
The cherub has erectile dysfunction
because genital herpes.

Hope

I feed the claw game
a dollar.

I feed the claw game
a dollar.

Behind glass
there's this plushie eggplant
with button eyes
you'd love.

I feed the claw game
a dollar.

Made in the USA
Middletown, DE
10 March 2025

72453592R00042